TRANSFORM
YOUR CHILD'S PRAYER LIFE
In Thirty Days

May God Bless You

Hazel Henry

TRANSFORM
YOUR CHILD'S PRAYER LIFE
In Thirty Days
A PRAYER JOURNAL

HAZEL HENRY

A Division of WINEPRESS PUBLISHING

Pleasant Word (a division of WinePress Publishing, PO Box 428, Enumclaw, WA 98022) functions only as book publisher. As such, the ultimate design, content, editorial accuracy, and views expressed or implied in this work are those of the author.

ISBN 13: 978-1-4141-1123-0
ISBN 10: 1-4141-1123-1
Library of Congress Catalog Card Number: 2007907695

This prayer journal is dedicated to all God's children young and old throughout the world. I want to thank my grandchildren, Frank, Annika and Ayianna who permitted me to teach them how to pray, and from this evolved the children's book "Transforming Your Child's Prayer Life in 30 Days." Thanks to Jan Fautheree who shared the "ACT" method of praying which got me off to the finishing line and for her son who is in the "act" of prayer daily. Thanks to the Gensolin's children who talk to God often in prayer as they are growing up. Thanks to the Karr's children who are really just learning to pray.

Much thanks goes to Amy Watkins, my inspiration and editor, to Brent and Kim Watkins for the tremendous support given to me, to Veronica Barnes who keeps me on task, and to Monica Preddie with her proofing skills and encouragement all along the way. A lot of thanks go to Owen Jolly, my illustrator whose talent has added much to make the journal "child friendly." But most of all I want to thank God for laying this "little" burden on my heart regarding prayer to get it out to His children.

CONTENTS

Day 1

LEARNING TO PRAY

One day He was praying in a certain place. When He finished, one of His disciples said, Master, teach us to pray just as John taught his disciples. So He said, When you pray, say Father, reveal who you are. Set the world right. Keep us alive with three square meals. Keep us forgiven with you and forgiving others. Keep us safe from ourselves and the Devil.

—Luke 11:1-4 *(The Message)*

Sometimes it helps to follow an easy plan when learning to pray. Jesus taught His disciples a simple prayer when they asked Him for help. When we pray we can **ASK** Jesus to help us with things we are worried about. We need to **CONFESS** the things we have done wrong and ask for Jesus' forgiveness. We should always **THANK** Him for the ways He

1

blesses us. Spend time praising Him for the ways you see Him working in your world.

This simple plan gives us direction when we are learning to pray. When we ACT in prayer we begin to build a friendship with Jesus that will fill that empty place we feel without Him. So, for the purposes of this book, we will use this simple plan as we learn about prayer and build a friendship with Jesus.

Application

Have you ever had a friend who moved away or was gone for a long time? How did you stay friends?

How could you do some of these things with your friend Jesus?

ACT

It's your turn. Ask Jesus about the things on your heart, Confess the things you've done wrong and Thank Him for His blessings.

Ask:

Confess:

Thank:

Journal Entry

_____

_____

_____

_____

_____

_____

_____

_____

_____

_____

_____

_____

_____

_____

_____

_____

_____

_____

_____

_____

_____

FRIENDSHIP WITH GOD

There is a friend who sticks closer than a brother.

—Proverbs 18:24

When Jesus created this world He desired friendship with His creation. He created in you a need for a relationship with Him. When we don't fill that need with Jesus, we feel empty and lonely. One way to fill that space with Jesus is to talk to Him and listen to Him talk to us. This is the beginning of a relationship. When you make a new friend at school or in your neighborhood it is important to spend time with your new friend. By spending time talking and playing with your new friend, you get to know each other. It works the same way with Jesus: the more time we spend with Him the better we know Him and the more friendship we have with Him. So let's explore ways to spend time with Jesus as we learn to pray and build a friendship with Jesus, our Creator.

Application

When have you felt empty or lonely?

What are some things you do that help you make friends with new people?

1.
2.
3.

How could you do something similar with Jesus?

ACT

Ask: Jesus, I'm empty when I don't spend time with you. Please fill me with You because I want to be Your special friend.

Confess: I don't always want to spend time with You and I find so many things taking my attention away from You. Please forgive me for putting my selfish heart first and help me set special time aside for You.

Thank: Thank You for wanting to spend time with me. Thank You for being patient with me as I learn how to talk and spend time with You.

Journal Entry

_____

_____

_____

_____

_____

_____

_____

_____

_____

_____

_____

_____

_____

_____

_____

_____

_____

_____

_____

_____

Day 3

THE PURPOSE OF PRAYER

For God has put it into their hearts to fulfill His purpose, to be of one mind...

—Revelation 17:17

Our best Friend, Jesus has one purpose in His mind for us: to be connected to Him at all times. In a practical way, I think of having the toaster plugged in to make my toast for breakfast. If the toaster is unplugged, then there is no toast. Prayer has the creative power through the Holy Spirit to keep us "plugged in" to the Source of our power: Jesus. When we wake up each morning we can immediately plug into the Source of power through prayer just by thanking Him for waking us up. As you jump out of bed, say, "Praise the Lord, praise His name." That will get you plugged in first thing.

During the day we can stay plugged in by checking with Him during everything we do. All we need to do is keep talking to Him as if we were talking to our best friend in school or church. Spending time with your friends on the playground is fun, and spending time with Jesus can be fun as you tell Him your deepest secrets. You can be sure that your secrets are safe with Jesus.

Application

What can I do to make sure that I stay plugged in to Jesus all day long?

1.
2.
3.

ACT

Ask: Jesus, please help me to stay connected with You through prayer. Help me to remember to seek Your help at every step that I take.

Confess: I confess my lack of power and strength when I forget to remain plugged into the Source of power to take me through the day.

Thank: Thank You for living in me today. Thank You for reminding me to talk to You. Thank You for helping me to drink from Your fountain of love each day so that I can remain connected to You.

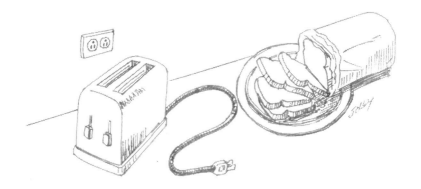

Journal Entry

_____

_____

_____

_____

_____

_____

_____

_____

_____

_____

_____

_____

_____

_____

_____

_____

_____

_____

PRAYER STARTS WITH GOD

In the same way the Spirit also comes to help
us, weak as we are. For we do not know how
we ought to pray; the Spirit Himself pleads with
God for us in groans that words cannot express.
And God, who sees into our hearts, knows what
the thought of the Spirit is; because the Spirit
pleads with God on behalf of His people and in
accordance with His will.

—Romans 8:26-27 (TEV)

As a child I really believed that prayer started with
me. My mom and dad taught me to pray, but as
I got older I wanted to pray by myself, just as you
are doing. I was the one kneeling with eyes closed
and speaking the words with my mom or dad's help,
at first, and then on my own. I was the one thinking up things to pray for and about. I was the one

waiting for God's answer. I would pray for my dog, Hitler. I thought I had to get God's attention. I can even remember shouting with hands waving, "God! Are you up there? Please listen to me!" I must have thought God was deaf. Prayer soon became boring to me. I found that I could not think up enough things to pray for.

As I grew older, I learned that I was wrong. God knows that we aren't able to pray without His help. The Holy Spirit, Jesus' special helper, is sent to help us in our weakness to teach us how to pray. Prayer does not start with me, but with God. This truth has changed my prayer life forever, and it will change yours.

I thank God that He is the one who prompts us to pray, that He moves upon our minds to talk to Him. He gives us prayer ideas that pop up in our brains like light bulbs. Imagine, He holds out His promises and we claim them in prayer. That is truly awesome! God is at work in all our praying. He works to make His will known to us so that we will ask for the very things He longs to give, and that is really cool!

Application

Did you ever think that when you got up in the morning or when you were going to bed at night and you knelt beside your bed that this prayer time started with you?

Name some of the ideas that the Holy Spirit has put in your mind to pray for?

1.
2.
3.

Did you find anything in the text listed that will allow you to see that prayer begins with God?

ACT

Ask: Dear Jesus, I am asking You to open my mind so that I can understand that You are the One who directs me what to pray.

Confess: I confess that I don't understand how prayer can start with Someone I cannot see, but because the Word of God says so, I will believe. Please forgive my unbelief.

Thank: Thank You, God, for showing me in Your Word that prayer does start with You, and I am thankful that You are still willing to teach your children how to pray.

Journal Entry

_____

_____

_____

_____

_____

_____

_____

_____

_____

_____

_____

_____

_____

_____

_____

_____

_____

_____

_____

Day 5

I DON'T KNOW WHAT TO PRAY

In the same way the Spirit also comes to help us, weak as we are. For we do not know how we ought to pray; the Spirit Himself pleads with God for us in groans that words cannot express. And God, who sees into our hearts, knows what the thought of the Spirit is; because the Spirit pleads with God on behalf of His people and in accordance with His will.

—Romans 8:26, 27 (TEV)

Together Jesus, God and the Holy Spirit are what we call the Trinity or "Godhead." The Holy Spirit is the one who makes our prayers possible. There are times when we don't know what to pray about. When you are visiting with your friends it's helpful when they can start some conversations and help you share with them. Our text today says that when we don't know what to pray God's Spirit does the same thing by impressing us to pray for what we really need. When we don't know what to pray the Holy Spirit is there showing God's will to us in the Bible and bringing God's prayer concerns to life within us. The Holy Spirit, God's sweet Presence prompts us to pray. He moves upon our minds and reminds us to talk with Him. He even gives us ideas to pray about. It is our responsibility to respond.

Application

Share a time that you didn't know what to pray about?

Ask Jesus to help you know what to pray about (this is especially important when confessing our wrongs and asking Jesus for forgiveness).

What has Jesus impressed on your mind to pray about?

ACT

Ask: Jesus, please impress upon my mind the things I need to pray for and about.

Confess: I do confess that my mind is so full of other stuff that I don't know what to pray for.

Thank: Thank You, for reminding me that I can talk to You about anything because You're my best friend.

Journal Entry

_____

_____

_____

_____

_____

_____

_____

_____

_____

_____

_____

_____

_____

_____

_____

_____

_____

_____

_____

_____

Day 6

THE NUDGING OF THE HOLY SPIRIT

If ye then, being evil, know how to give good gifts unto your children; how much more shall your heavenly Father give the Holy Spirit to them that ask Him?

—Luke 11:13

We have talked about the Holy Spirit being the third person of the Godhead. He is the one that Jesus sent to us after He went back to heaven to prepare a place for us. He is the one who inspires us to do things for others. He nudges us in small, quiet ways through things that happen to us and through opening our eyes to the needs of others around us.

God speaks to us through the Holy Spirit, helping us to search our hearts, which are really our minds, which are really our brains. The Holy Spirit can bring us into real friendship with the Father, Jesus and Himself. We can ask God to give us the Holy Spirit every day when we wake up. During the day, we can ask Him to continue to be with us and guide us into what is true all throughout the day. We should even pray for the Holy Spirit to be with us during our sleep time.

Application

Have you ever wondered who the Holy Spirit is? Have you ever felt the need for the Holy Spirit?

What does the Holy Spirit do since He is referred to as a Spirit? I will give you an example and you do the rest.

1. He guides us into what is true.
2.
3.

How can the Holy Spirit become an important part of your life?

ACT

Ask: Jesus, I need the Holy Spirit to dwell within me today. I don't know how to have Him do this, so I am asking You, my best friend, to allow Him to be an important part of my life today.

Confess: I am not sure who the Holy Spirit is, but I know I need Him in my life to take me through each day. I certainly don't know how this is done, so I confess my lack of understanding and ask you to help me to ask continually for the Holy Spirit to be with me everywhere I go.

Thank: Thank You for wanting to give me this gift of the Holy Spirit and I accept Him in my life. Thank You for the promise to give the Holy Spirit to those who ask, even to children who are seeking.

Journal Entry

_____

_____

_____

_____

_____

_____

_____

_____

_____

_____

_____

_____

_____

_____

_____

_____

_____

_____

_____

_____

Day 7

LISTENING TO GOD'S WORD

O Lord, hear! O Lord, forgive! O Lord, listen and act! Do not delay for Your own sake, my God, for our city and Your people are called by Your name.

—Daniel 8:19

Since prayer starts with God, our first order of business is to learn how to listen to the whisperings and nudging of His Holy Spirit so that we can tune our hearts to respond to His promptings. The Holy Spirit doesn't usually speak to us in a loud voice; instead, He uses what the Bible calls a "still, small voice." To hear it, we have to listen carefully. We can do that by turning off the TV, taking a break from video games and music and quietly reading and thinking about God's Word. God listens carefully to our prayers, so we should be willing to listen carefully to Him.

Application

Have you ever heard God's voice, God speaking directly to you?

Name some things you can do to help you listen better to the voice of God.

1.
2.
3.

How can you make asking for the Holy Spirit something you do every day?

ACT

Ask: Jesus, please help me to listen to You every day by being quiet and thinking on Your Word.

Confess: I confess to You that I don't always know how to listen. I ask Your forgiveness and continue to plead with you to help me in this way.

Thank: Thank You for being patient with me as I learn to listen to You more and more every day. I thank You for reminding me to turn off the TV and stop thinking on my video games as I spend time with You. I thank You for helping me to be **present** in my worship time with You in my mind as well as in my body.

Journal Entry

_____

_____

_____

_____

_____

_____

_____

_____

_____

_____

_____

_____

_____

_____

_____

_____

_____

_____

_____

_____

Day 8

LISTENING MORE TO GOD AND TO OTHERS

Why do you not understand My speech? Because you are not able to listen to My word.
—John 8:43

Someone observed that we need to listen twice as much as we talk. I wonder why? I see that God made each one of us with two ears and one mouth. That should give us a clue to listen more and talk less.

Real listening seems to have taken wings and flown away, for nearly no one listens any more, but here is a story of a man who listened carefully. A pastor related this incident that took place in his church. A disheveled man apparently walked in off the street right in the middle of the sermon. The visitor started looking for an empty seat in the back, but failing to find one, he walked slowly down the aisle searching. Still not finding an empty seat, he kept on going to the front of the sanctuary. By this time the stranger had produced a lot of commotion among the worshipers. When he reached the front and still no one had offered him a seat, he simply squatted down right there in the aisle in front of the entire stunned congregation.

As he sat there listening to the rest of the sermon, an old deacon approached the strange and unexpected visitor. *What will the deacon do?* the people wondered. *Will he usher him out, or will he...?* To the amazement of everyone present, the old deacon touched the man's shoulder and squatted down right next to him. This is truly what it means to sympathize. That is the best way of listening.

Application

Have you ever taken the time to listen carefully to a friend, brother or sister?

How can you listen to your best friend, Jesus each day?

1. Read my Bible and listen to what it tells me to do.
2.
3.

ACT

Ask: I am asking You to help me to listen to You more carefully. I ask that You will help me to do what I hear You telling me to do.

Confess: I confess that I don't pay much attention to others only to myself, but with Your help this action will change.

Thank: I thank You, Jesus, for helping me to become a more careful listener, making You first in my life, listening to others and allowing You to take care of me.

Journal Entry

Day 9

OUR SPECIAL PRIVILEGE

Therefore confess your sins to each other and
pray for each other so that you may be healed.
The prayer of a righteous man is powerful and
effective.

—James 5:16

When we listen to our friends' problems and
listen to the prayer ideas the Holy Spirit puts
into our minds, we can take part in a special privilege: praying for other people. When we pray for
others God pours His special blessing out on them
just as if they were praying for themselves. Isn't that
cool? You can pray for your family, your teachers,
your neighbors, and God will bless them.

This kind of praying is called "intercession"—a
big word that just means "to pray for someone else."
When you know of someone who is having troubles,

pray for them. When your friend is sick and you want to do something special for them, pray. When your grandma or grandpa is far away and you miss them, pray for them. There are so many wonderful times that we can put people in the care of Jesus, just by asking Him to bless them.

Application

Who would you like to place in the care of Jesus today?

What is happening in their lives that Jesus could help with?

ACT

Ask: Dear Jesus, help me to understand the awesome privilege I have in being able to tell You what I have done wrong and be forgiven. I know some of my friends are having a hard time with their friendship with You, and as You help me, I will be able to help them.

Confess: I confess my inability to understand and ask Your forgiveness.

Thank: I thank You, Jesus, for helping me to be bold and bring all my problems and the problems of my friends to You. Thank You for loving me in spite of myself.

Journal Entry

_____

_____

_____

_____

_____

_____

_____

_____

_____

_____

_____

_____

_____

_____

_____

_____

_____

_____

_____

_____

_____

WHAT IS INTERCESSION?

And Jesus said to his disciples, "Suppose one of you should go to a friend's house at midnight and say, 'Friend, let me borrow three loaves of bread. A friend of mine who is on a trip has just come to my house, and I don't have any food for him!' And suppose your friend should answer from inside, 'Don't bother me! The door is already locked, and my children and I are in bed. I can't get up and give you anything.' Well, what then? I tell you that even if he will not get up and give you the bread because you are his friend, yet he will get up and give you everything you need because you are not ashamed to keep on asking."

—Luke 11:5-8 (TEV)

We need to pray for ourselves so that we may receive all that God intends for us to have, but as an act of self-giving, we also need to pray for other people. When we shift our focus from praying for ourselves to praying for other people, that is intercession.

The person in our verse for today is the friend-in-the-middle. He has a friend in need that has come in the middle of the night, and he also has a friend with bread. He has no food to give his friend in need, so he goes to his other friend and begs boldly and shamelessly till he receives what he wants for his friend in need.

Look carefully and you will see that the person in the middle, the go-between, is the intercessor. He is seriously asking the one who has much to give to share with the one who has nothing. So it should be with us when we go to God on behalf of another person. Intercessors are workers or laborers for God.

Application

Who can you become an in-between for?

1.
2.
3.

Other than family members name three people that you can intercede for?

1.
2.
3.

ACT

Ask: Dear Jesus, please help me to love to pray for my parents and for my friends. I am also asking You to help me to include my teachers and my neighbors when I come to You.

Confess: I confess my failure to intercede faithfully for those around me who are in need of my prayers.

Thank: I thank You for providing this way of using me to pray for others. I want to take the time right now to pray for those who come to mind. Thank You for helping me to make a list of all those for whom I will bring to You daily.

Journal Entry

_____

_____

_____

_____

_____

_____

_____

_____

_____

_____

_____

_____

_____

_____

_____

_____

_____

_____

_____

_____

BEARING OTHERS' BURDENS

Come to Me, all you who labor and are heavy laden, and I will give you rest.

—Matthew 11:28

B ecause God is love and prayer starts with God, He puts the idea in our minds that we should pray for others all the time. This is what your parents or grandparents might call the "burden" that God places in our hearts to pray for others. In response to our prayers for others He can pour out blessings on them. Just think of God pouring out His blessings on those you are praying for just like you pour milk on your cereal!

This principle motivated Jesus' entire life on earth, and it should motivate each of us. He loved to bear the burdens of those who were suffering. Jesus could have told those who came to Him with their heavy burdens, "Go to My Father," but instead He told them to come to Him and He would take care of the problem. That is how we should be, especially if we want to be just like Jesus. We are to make sure that we are following His example, so let's see what we need to do.

Application

Name some friends or family that you have prayed for and for what you prayed. Did you get an answer?

Let's look at one example and then you may choose to write your own. Your grandma is always losing her eye glasses. That is the "burden" Jesus puts on your heart. You respond to His suggestion by praying for God to help your grandma find her glasses. When you talk to Grandma the next time, you ask, "Did you find your glasses, Grandma?" She answers, "Yes, dear, were you praying for me?"

Can you ask Jesus for something like this?

Imagine that your friend has lost his/her cat or dog. What encouraging things could you do to help your friend?

1.
2.
3.

ACT

Ask: I need Your help, precious Jesus, to be able to see the burdens that my friends or others are carrying. Help me to do just what You would do to ease their sorrow, their pain or wipe their tears.

Confess: I confess to You that most of the time I have my eyes on myself and not on others. Touch my eyes so that I may begin to see as You see, so that I can do just what You would do.

Thank: Thank You, Jesus, for allowing me to see how others are having a hard time, and thank You for the help You promised in Your Word so that I can be just like You.

Journal Entry

_____

_____

_____

_____

_____

_____

_____

_____

_____

_____

_____

_____

_____

_____

_____

_____

_____

_____

_____

_____

_____

$\mathcal{D}\,a\,y$ 1 2

JESUS IS OUR
INTERCESSOR

It is part of God's plan to grant us, in answer
to the prayer of faith, that which He would not
bestow did we not thus ask.
    —*Great Controversy, by E. G. White*, p. 525

This truth is just hitting me like a bolt out of the
blue. My friend, Jesus is saying to your mom,
dad or grandma, "When your children or grandchildren go to school each morning, they are heading
out into battle." Your mom and dad are committed to
praying for you with uplifted hands so that you can
win the battle with the help of Jesus. Your parents
will keep you in prayer before God for they know
that if they stop praying for you, the battle will be
lost. Your pastors also lift up their hands in prayer
to God asking Him to keep you safe from the evil
that surrounds you. When they do this the church

grows strong and the gates of hell cannot prevail against it. Jesus Himself has even promised to be an intercessor for you. You can ask Jesus to pray for you and with you.

Even though we are young, let us commit ourselves to lift up our hands in prayer in our neighborhood for protection so that the powers of darkness may be pushed back. Let us also be committed to walk through our neighborhood praying for the people in each house and asking God to make our neighborhood a place where Christ loves to walk.

Application

When was the last time you prayed for someone?

Have you seen or heard your parents, grandparents, teachers or friends praying for you?

Can you think of something you can ask Jesus to do for you today?

ACT

Ask: Dear Jesus, please help me to pray more often for my mom and dad and for my friends. Please help me to remember to pray for my pastors and teachers as well.

Confess: I confess to You that I keep forgetting to bring my friends and family to You. Please forgive me for I know that You will hear my prayers and protect and guide those whom I present to You.

Thank: I give You thanks and praise for all that You do for me daily and I thank You for guiding me into a life of prayer for myself and my friends.

Journal Entry

_____

_____

_____

_____

_____

_____

_____

_____

_____

_____

_____

_____

_____

_____

_____

_____

_____

_____

How Do I Know God Hears Me?

If you believe, you will receive whatever you ask for in prayer.

—Matthew 21:22

The surest way to know that God hears you when you pray is to make sure you are praying "in His will." When we tune in to Jesus by reading the Bible (His Words) we know what He wants for us. When we tune in to a radio we have to be on the right wavelength to hear anything clearly. The Bible gives us direction and knowledge so that we know what to "tune in to" when we pray. The more we know about what God says in His Word the more we are able to tune in to His whispers and prompt-ings in our hearts. When we are tuned in to Him, we know the kind of things to bring to Him in prayer.

We can even ask Him to teach us what to pray, to help us understand what He wants, to feel His burdens and see what He sees. When we are tuned in to Jesus, praying His will, we can claim the promise of Matthew 21:22: **"You will receive whatever you ask for in prayer."**

Application

Spend some time talking to Jesus about what you should pray for. What did Jesus reveal to your heart?

Pray.

ACT

Ask: Dear Jesus, please help me to read Your Word and learn what You want me to do. Please help me to be faithful so that I can go in the right direction.

Confess: I confess that I don't understand a lot of what I read and so I just pass it over instead of asking an older person to help me. Please help me to do better day after day.

Thank: Thank You for providing a way for me to know that You hear and that You answer me. I do know that You don't always say "yes." I know that You say "no" sometimes and other times You allow me to "wait." Help me to be thankful for the answer that I receive.

Journal Entry

_____

_____

_____

_____

_____

_____

_____

_____

_____

_____

_____

_____

_____

_____

_____

_____

_____

_____

_____

CONFIDENCE WITH GOD

Jesus answered them, have faith in God…For this reason I tell you when you pray ask for something, believe that you have received it, and you will be given whatever you ask for.

—Mark 11:22-24 (TEV)

It is better to trust in the Lord than to put confidence in man.

—Psalm 118:8

Prayer without faith is incomplete and, therefore, not true prayer. Faith is the assurance of things we hope for, the certainty of things we cannot see. When your mom, your dad, or your grandparents promise you something, you believe that you will get it. Sometimes you even thank them for it ahead of time. Let me tell you my version of a story that I read some long time ago. Once, a young boy's grandmother promised him a photo album for Christmas, and he trusted her so much that he thanked her for it. However, at Christmas time the long looked for package did not come. His mom said, "Son, grandma may have forgotten to get you the album."

"No, Mom, it will come," he said. "My grandma has never failed me yet."

Another week and still another, but no album. His mother kept at him telling him that his grandmother had forgotten. "You know, she is getting old and could have forgotten."

The young boy got out his pencil and paper and wrote to his grandmother asking about his gift. In no time at all the answer came: "Dear grandson, I have not forgotten your gift. As a matter of fact, I got it and sent it out to have something special done on it as a surprise. When it came back to me, it was not to my satisfaction, so I had to send it back. You know grandma would not let you down. As soon as I have your album and it is to my satisfaction I will send it to you."

The boy was so pleased, that he ran to his mother, "I told you, I told you, my grandma has not forgotten," and he showed her the letter. O what faith, what belief! In a little while the mail carrier brought the long awaited gift, and the boy was happy that he knew his grandmother was faithful to her word.

We can trust God because He keeps His promises. We can depend on Him because He is faithful to His Word. One of God's promises is that He will hear us when we pray. We can have confidence that He will keep that promise. If you want to grow strong in prayer, grow strong in faith. If you want to grow strong in faith, get to know God better. If you want to get to know God better, spend time with Him reading His Word and listening to Him. Remember that God answers in three ways, so you must be on the look out for answers: Yes, No, and Wait.

Application

Do you have faith in Jesus like the little boy had in his grandmother?

How can you know for sure that your prayers are being heard?

Write down your own story of faith.

ACT

ASK: Jesus, please help me to have the confidence I need in Your Word to know that whatever You say, You will do. May my faith be like yeast that transforms dough into bread. Please transform me through Your Word and with the faith that you are giving me.

Confess: I am sorry, Lord, for not having the trust that I need in You. Please forgive me and help me to just believe what You say.

Thank: I thank You for teaching me that I can trust Your Word. So please help me to do this each and every day. I thank You for Your promise that You will give a measure of faith to everyone. Thank You for helping me to improve on this gift.

Journal Entry

_____

_____

_____

_____

_____

_____

_____

_____

_____

_____

_____

_____

_____

_____

_____

_____

_____

_____

_____

_____

Day 15

THE NEED FOR A CLEAN HEART

If I had ignored my sins, the Lord would not have listened to me. But God has indeed heard me; he has listened to my prayer.

—Psalm 66:18, 19

Sin in our lives prevents our prayers from being heard. Many times when our prayers are not answered, we put the blame on God, but the blame is really with us. We might think we are keeping our sins hidden, but God sees clearly and knows our hearts and our sins.

When wrong doing blocks our prayers, the real problem is not that we have done wrong but that we have not repented or felt really sorry for what we have done. We haven't asked God's forgiveness. It is only un-confessed sins, cherished in our hearts that prevent our prayers from being heard. Forgiven sin does not prevent our prayers from being heard.

Application

What way has God provided for us to have a clean heart?

What does the Bible have to say about our confession and forgiveness? You might want to look up 1 John 1:9.

ACT

Ask: Dear Jesus, please help me to remember that the first requirement for prayer is to confess whatever is in my heart that is not of God. I ask that You help me to accept Your forgiveness and be confident that You are hearing and answering my prayer.

Confess: I confess to You my carelessness in not praying and asking You for forgiveness. I confess that I feel afraid to look at the uneasy areas in my life for I may find a cherished sin there. Help me to look and, by Your grace to deal with it in Your way. As I confess my sins to You, I want to remember the confidence David had. He said, "God has surely listened and heard my voice in prayer."

Thank: I thank You, Lord, for Your gift of a new and clean heart. Please clear my record and give me a heart like Yours.

Journal Entry

_____

_____

_____

_____

_____

_____

_____

_____

_____

_____

_____

_____

_____

_____

_____

_____

_____

_____

_____

_____

_____

CELEBRATING GOD THROUGH PRAYER

I will always thank the Lord; I will never stop praising Him. I will praise Him for what He has done; may all who are oppressed listen and be glad! Proclaim with me the Lord's greatness; let us praise His name together.

—Psalm 34:1-3 (TEV)

Everybody loves to have a good time laughing, giving hugs, singing, and talking together. Our everyday living gives us plenty of chances to do just that. We are using a big word here: **celebrate**, which really means having a good time. There are wonderful and joyous times when we celebrate: at Christmas time, on our birthdays, on New Year, our parents' anniversaries, and at graduations. To celebrate also means "**to honor or praise publicly.**" We "celebrate"

Super Bowl athletes and even cartoon characters.

There is no better reason to celebrate than coming to know Jesus and be in His Presence. Our God deserves honor and praise more than anyone or anything else in the whole wide world. One great preacher asks us to "think magnificently of God." As you think magnificently of God, you call to your mind His greatness and goodness, and that gives each of us cause to celebrate.

Application

When did you last have a celebration with friends?

How could you do something similar with Jesus?

Name some things you could do to celebrate God's Presence in your life?

1.
2.
3.

ACT

Ask: Jesus, please teach me how to celebrate with You instead of wanting only to have fun with my friends all the time.

Confess: I confess my sin of gushing over things like Sponge Bob, the Super Bowl or Harry Potter.

Please forgive and help me to enjoy being with You instead of only things that are of little value to my coming home to live with You forever.

Thank: Thank You, Jesus, for wanting to teach me how to celebrate Your love and Your care. Thanks for Your patience as I learn new ways of celebrating with You.

Journal Entry

STILL CELEBRATING GOD THROUGH PRAYER

Blessed are those who dwell in Your house; they will still be praising You.

—Psalm 84:4

We all need to give God all the honor and the praise for He is the One who has made us and causes to grow and develop into young adults. Let us not forget the source of all good things: **GOD.**

In celebrating God, we are seeing God for who He is. God's glory is His majestic splendor shining out so it can be seen and known by all. When we are in that mode of glorifying God we are not giving Him anything. We can't add luster to Him, just as we can't add glory or splendor to a sunrise or a sunset. We can only look on in awe and wonder at the beauty and glory of the Lord.

Set aside some time today to gaze on God's goodness and love for you. God shows His love for us to the point of overflowing. Walk out into your garden or backyard and listen to the birds: they are singing praises to the God you love. Allow your mind to dwell on several of God's attributes like His love, His wisdom and His power. Take time to look at a flower and see God's goodness there.

Application

Have you ever had an opportunity to give God all the glory and honor that you can?

Name some things you can do to give God honor and praise in celebrating His love for you.

1.
2.
3.

ACT

Ask: Jesus, I am asking You to help me to know how to praise You better. I need to know how to bring glory and honor to Your name. Thank You!

Confess: I confess that there has been very little heartfelt praise for You coming from me. Please forgive me as I will do better each day with Your wonderful help.

Thank: Thank You, Jesus, for being patient and kind to me and for helping me to let Your glory shine through my life today as I give You my heart.

Journal Entry

_____

_____

_____

_____

_____

_____

_____

_____

_____

_____

_____

_____

_____

_____

_____

_____

_____

_____

_____

_____

$\mathcal{D}\,a\,y\;\;1\,8$

GOD NEEDS OUR PRAYERS

Moses said to Joshua, pick out some men to go
and fight the Amalekites tomorrow. I will stand
on top of the hill holding the stick that God told
me to carry…As long as Moses held up his arms,
the Israelites won but when he put his arms down
the Amalekites started winning.
—Exodus 17:9, 11 (TEV)

The Israelites faced a crisis in battle, so Joshua and
the army went out to fight while their leader,
Moses, went up on top of a hill to pray. When Moses'
praying hands were held up the Israelites won, but
when his praying hands got tired and he put them
down, the enemy began winning.

Some people think that we need more education,
more books, more ideas, and even more strategies to
do something for God. The Bible tells us that what

we need is hands uplifted in prayer. Did you know that our lives can become a prayer? When we talk to God, He lets us know what is on His agenda. Truly awesome! We are invited by Jesus to pray for each other, this will help us not to become discouraged. It would be nice if everyone would see the need for uplifted hands in prayer to God so that He could work His purposes through us.

Let us try to stand outside our home or apartment, look up, and look around. May be you can see some of the damage that Satan is trying to do to God's people. Lift up your hands or your hearts in prayer over your neighborhood. Imagine God, in response to your prayers, moving to frustrate what Satan is trying to do.

Application

Why do you think God allowed His people who include you and me, to suffer defeat when there was no prayer? Do you think that God was teaching His people that He chooses to move in response to prayer and that He will not move without it?

Where do you think in God's kingdom are people winning against the powers of darkness because of your prayers?

Are there places you are seeing where they appear to be losing because there is little or no prayer?

What kind of things do you think God might want you to do on your street in response to your prayers?

ACT

Ask: Jesus, I know You are fully able to work without my prayers, but because You are so good You choose to work through my prayers. Please help me to remember and pray often to You. Help me to be Your prayer partner as I pray for my parents, friends and neighbors. Please help me to understand why my little prayers or even the prayers of my parents are so important to You.

Confess: I confess the lack of prayer in my life, but with Your help, and with my learning to listen, things will be better starting today.

Thank: Thank You for calling me into a working partnership with You. Thank You for choosing to work for and through me. Please help me to remain thankful on a daily basis and to know that God is interested in talking and working with me daily.

Journal Entry

_____

_____

_____

_____

_____

_____

_____

_____

_____

_____

_____

_____

_____

_____

_____

_____

_____

_____

_____

GOD WELCOMES CHILDREN TO HIS THRONE ROOM

Let us have confidence, then, and approach God's throne, where there is grace. There we will receive mercy and find grace to help us just when we need it.

—Hebrews 4:16 (TEV)

God is calling you to come into His throne room where He is and this is really the foundation of prayer. All of us as children must come to the throne. Even more wonderful is that we are welcome there.

"The Holy Spirit of God will impress the lessons upon the receptive minds of the children that they may grasp the ideas of Bible truth in their simplicity. And the Lord will give an experience to these children in missionary lines. He will suggest to them lines of thought that even the teachers did not have.

The children who are properly instructed will be witnesses for the truth.

"Work as if you were working for your life to save children from being drowned in the polluting, corrupting influences of this life." (Taken from E.G. White's *Child Guidance,* p. 309). This is wonderful that the Holy Spirit will also teach us how to pray.

Application

What do you think: is it a privilege or a right to enter God's throne room? Keep in mind that the one we approach is the sovereign, all-powerful, holy ruler of the universe. What a privilege!

How do we find entrance into the throne room of God?

Here are some things God does to welcome us:

1. He extends a hand of welcome to us.
2. The door is wide open, we may enter.
3. God is expecting us and glad to see us

ACT

Ask: Jesus, I am asking You to help me to see through Your eyes the throne room. I am visualizing You high and lifted upon Your throne. Your glory fills the room just like sunshine pouring through my window. In my imagination I can see the angels all around. I am feeling overwhelmed with fear and dread, except for one thing: God recognizes me. He even knows my name. He looks at me, smiles, and extends a hand of welcome.

Confess: I confess that I was frightened when You spoke to me. I can even remember Your question: **"Tell Me, why have you come?"** I nearly forgot. I then fell at Your feet and poured out my joys and sorrows and told You I came to be with my best Friend and I want to stay right here at His feet.

Thank: I want to thank You for who You are to me and for making even children happy and welcome in this special room.

Journal Entry

_____

_____

_____

_____

_____

_____

_____

_____

_____

_____

_____

_____

_____

_____

_____

_____

_____

_____

_____

Day 20

ADOPTED AS SONS AND DAUGHTERS

Having predestined us to adoption as sons by Jesus Christ to Himself, according to the good pleasure of His will.

—Ephesians 1:5

I find it quite exciting to know that I am not only a friend of Jesus, but His Father has adopted me as His child and now Jesus is my very own brother. Besides that, I am now royalty. I have a place in the royal family; I am a child of the King of Heaven because Jesus has made me acceptable to God.

When we come to the throne of grace, we are coming to talk to our Father. We can confidently bring our concerns, our joys and our sorrows to Him, and we can come as intercessors for others.

Application

Have you been able to tell Jesus your needs, wants and desires for your family, friends, and neighbors recently?

During the course of this week, bring a friend to Jesus and watch as He answers your prayers.

ACT

Ask: Dear Jesus, please help me to bring my concerns to You. I need Your help in my daily school work, in doing my chores, and in praying for my friends.

Confess: I confess that I don't always want to do my chores, and sometimes I forget to pray for my friends. Please forgive me and help me to do better every day.

Thank: I thank You, God, for allowing me the awesome privilege of being your son or daughter and for Jesus who is my elder brother. Help me to honor this privilege every day.

Journal Entry

_____

_____

_____

_____

_____

_____

_____

_____

_____

_____

_____

_____

_____

_____

_____

_____

_____

_____

_____

_____

_____

_____

Day 21

THE LIFE THAT CAN PRAY

We have confidence before God and receive from
Him anything we ask, because we obey His com-
mands and do what pleases him.
                              —1 John 3:21, 22 (NKJV)

In his book *"If My People Pray,"* Randy Maxwell
talks of prayer as exercise. He says that many of
us view prayer the same way we do exercise—it's
a drag. We know exercise is good for us. It relieves
stress. It improves circulation. It strengthens the
heart. It improves physical appearance. In spite of
all these good things that exercise does for us, we
would sometimes rather keep lifting a fork to our
mouths than lift weights.

People who enjoy exercising are found in the
fitness clubs. They play racquetball, they swim laps,
they run track, and they ride stationary bikes. Their

hearts and lungs are in great shape. They are in good shape, but people call them fanatics. Sadly, this is how many people view prayer. We know prayer is good for us. Deep down in our spirits, we know that prayer is important—that it strengthens our relationship with God, relieves stress, boosts our faith and is the source of unlimited spiritual power—but sometimes we would rather keep doing the things that weaken us than perform the exercise of prayer that will make us strong.

Application

How can you use exercise as a model for your prayer life?

1. As I run around for exercise, I can ask Jesus to help me to run my Bible verses through my mind to keep my mind spiritually fit.
2. As I keep my heart and lungs fit through exercise, I can keep my spiritual mind fit by asking for the Breath of Life (the Holy Spirit) to flow through me daily.
3. Your turn!

ACT

Ask: Dear Jesus, I am asking You to help my whole life will to be a prayer. As I walk, run, skip and jump I want to be doing it with You. Please help me to make You a part of each activity that I do.

Confess: I confess that I seem to forget what I need to be doing with You when I am doing my daily activities. Please forgive me.

Thank: Thank You for being my God and for helping me to be obedient.

Journal Entry

_____

_____

_____

_____

_____

_____

_____

_____

_____

_____

_____

_____

_____

_____

_____

_____

_____

_____

_____

_____

$\mathcal{D}ay$ 22

IS YOUR PRAYER LIFE A BORE?

Keep watching and pray that you may not enter into temptation…

—Matthew 26:41

Can you believe that Jesus wants your young life to be one of prayer? He wants you to keep watching, to keep praying so that temptations will not overtake you. It does not mean that you always have to be on your knees, but you can always have an attitude of prayer. As you move about your day, you can pray about the things you see and the things you do. I am sure that you do not want to view prayer as boring, painful, or just too much trouble, for you know the desirable benefits that prayer brings into your life.

You can become a powerful young *pray-er* by spending time with the Lord and spending time in

His Word. You can become more effective by being obedient. My grandchildren's mom was obedient to God while she was driving on a busy highway. Her truck began to shake and she heard a voice saying, "Move over to the right lane." In obedience, she moved over immediately. As soon as she got into the right lane, her left front tire flew off on the busy highway, but she was able to stop the truck without incident. The tire could not be found, but she and her children were safe. She thanked God for helping her to listen to His voice, and for keeping her safe through her obedience to His voice. Prayer does matter, and it is within our reach whether we are children or adults.

Application

You can make Jesus delight in you by being obedient to His word. List three ways that you can have God delight in you.

1.
2.
3.

ACT

Ask: Dear Jesus, I am asking You to help me to spend more time with You by reading from Your Word and listening carefully to what You have to say so that I can bring You delight.

Confess: I confess that I sometimes forget to talk to You in prayer and I also forget to read from Your holy book. Please forgive me and by Your help I will be more obedient.

Thank: I give You thanks for all that You do for me on a daily basis. I want to thank You for Your written word and that You are offering it to me to guide my life daily.

Journal Entry

_____

_____

_____

_____

_____

_____

_____

_____

_____

_____

_____

_____

_____

_____

_____

_____

_____

_____

_____

_____

Praying in Jesus' Name

Until now you have not asked for anything in
my name. Ask and you will receive, and your
joy will be complete.

—John 16:24

By making the offer to us to pray in His name,
Jesus is offering an amazingly wonderful and
great privilege to us. It's like giving us a blank check
to be written and drawn on the bank of heaven for
any amount.

By doing this, He is putting great trust in us. He
is saying that His honor is safe in our hands. It is
as if He has put all His creation in our care. He is
asking us to take control over all His estate. We now
use this power through prayer. Through prayer we
ask God the Father for all we need in order to get
the job done. Through prayer we direct God's grace

and power to special locations where it is needed. Jesus knows that we will use it to bring glory and honor to His name.

Application

How do you understand the meaning of praying in the name of Jesus?

1. We are here authorized by Christ to be His representatives.
2. We do this because of who Jesus is and because He has given us the right to do so.

Think about the responsibility we have for building some part of Christ's kingdom by praying in His name and getting answers. Awesome!

ACT

Ask: Dear Jesus, I understand Your desire for me to ask for anything I want to accomplish for You in Your name. Help me to take this responsibility very seriously.

Confess: I confess any selfish praying that has not represented Your mind and has not been according to Your will. I am asking for anything You need in order to complete Your will in my life and in the world in which I live.

Thank: I thank You for the awesome privilege of praying in Your name and I am thankful that You will bring to my mind to seal my prayers with "in Jesus name." I love you Lord.

Journal Entry

_____

_____

_____

_____

_____

_____

_____

_____

_____

_____

_____

_____

_____

_____

_____

_____

_____

_____

_____

_____

Day 24

LET ME REST IN HIM

Take my yoke upon you, and lean of me; for I am meek and lowly in heart; and ye shall find rest unto your souls.

—Matthew 11:29

As we walk our life's journey in meekness and lowliness of heart, God does a work for each one of us that only He can do: give us true rest. Let us remember that as God that is working in us, giving us the strength and will to do His work, it is also His pleasure to give us rest. The Bible says it is God's "good pleasure" to have us abide in Christ and rest in His love. As we continue to rest in Him, we should let no one rob our souls of peace and restfulness, nor of the full assurance that we are accepted right now, just as we are.

You can apply God's promise of rest to your life. All God's promises are yours on the one condition that you follow the Lord's prescribed terms. Have you found rest for your soul? If not remember that "it is by learning the habits of Christ, His meekness, His lowliness, that self becomes transformed—by taking Christ's yoke upon you and then submitting to learn" (*Ye Shall Receive Power*, by E.G. White, pg. 62). Now is the time to take advantage of the secret of resting in His love by surrendering your ways to Him, making Christ's ways your ways. This will allow you to enjoy His perfect rest.

Application

Are you willing to let Jesus be your teacher? Then ask Him to do that for you.

ACT

Ask: Dear Jesus, I ask You to help me to surrender so that You can live in my human body. Abide in me and let me live in You so that I can enjoy true rest.

Confess: I confess that I have not always been willing to submit myself to Your training. With Your help I now submit myself to You so that You can work out the type of character that will have me transformed from the lower school to the higher grade.

Thank: I want to thank You for helping me to submit all things to You. I am consciously allowing Your life,

Your patience, Your longsuffering, Your forbearance, Your meekness, and Your lowliness to be worked out in my character, so that I can be one of those young people that rests in You.

Journal Entry

BEHOLD HIM DAILY

Look unto me, and be ye saved, all the ends of the
earth; for I am God, and there is none else.
—Isaiah 45:22

Let's take the time to look at Jesus. As the old
song goes, let's turn our eyes upon Jesus, look
full in His wonderful face so that the things of earth
will grow strangely dim in the light of His glory and
grace. As we look upon Jesus, concentrating on His
character and getting to know Him as our friend,
our faith grows strong with the love that He places
in our soul. It purifies our whole being! Through
faith the Holy Spirit works in our hearts to create
holiness within us, but this can only happen if we
allow the Holy Spirit to do His work. No one is
forced to look at Jesus, but the invitation is always

available to "look and live." Every day we must allow the Holy Spirit's influence to transform our hearts into a perfect picture of Jesus' righteous nature. As we grow in Christ and keep looking at Him, He will allow the Holy Spirit to elevate our taste, sanctify our heart, and ennoble our whole person.

My dear friend, let your soul look to Jesus. "Behold the Lamb of God, which taketh away the sin of the world" (John 1:29). As we look to Jesus, we will see that His love is without comparison. He has taken our place as sinners and has given us His perfection like a beautiful robe that covers us completely; all we have to do is allow Him to wrap us up in it.

Application

Have you taken the time to see your Savior today? Do so now; it will put a smile on Jesus' face.

Have you taken the time to see your Savior's pardoning love, the love that allows us to love Him and others in return? Take the time to do so now.

ACT

Ask: Dear Jesus, I ask You to help me to really "see" You today. Help me to realize that God "is faithful and just to forgive us our sins, and to cleanse us from all unrighteousness" (1 John 1:9). Please help me to reach from strength to greater strength and from grace to grace in You.

Confess: I confess my weakness, my unfaithfulness to Your love for me. Please forgive me and lead me into Your righteousness.

Thank: Thank you for teaching me Your will and Your way. I thank You for helping me to keep looking unto Jesus who will keep me faithful.

Journal Entry

_____

_____

_____

_____

_____

_____

_____

_____

_____

_____

_____

_____

_____

_____

_____

_____

_____

_____

_____

_____

Day 26

ALWAYS GROWING IN
MY PRAYER LIFE

But the path of the just is as the shining light, that
shineth more and more unto the perfect day.
—Proverbs 4:18

Compared to Jesus, we are all weak and puny,
even when we try our hardest to be strong,
but we don't have to remain small in our walk with
Christ. God promises that spiritual favor and power
will be provided for every true believer, and that
means you and me. As we exercise the ability which
God has given us, we learn and receive His strength.
We are like growing plants in the Lord's garden that
need daily water and plant food, and God is a good
gardener who knows what we need to grow spiritually. He gives us the spiritual fervor and power—like
the water and plant food we provide the plants in

our gardens—so that we can grow spiritually and blossom with faith and knowledge of our Lord and precious Savior.

We must have a constant supply of spiritual life. No halfway houses have been set along the way where we can put off our responsibility and rest by the wayside. Even when we're young, we must keep advancing heavenward, and as we do so we will develop solid characters. Otherwise our spiritual growth will wilt and die like a plant without water.

Application

Have you asked for the Holy Spirit to empower you so that you, in turn, will be able to share the light that He has given you? If this is your desire, then ask for the Holy Sprit to fill you.

Because of the promises of Christ, can you be sure that you will not "wilt"? He has promised to give you His Spirit; will you accept Him?

ACT

Ask: Dear Jesus, I ask You to water me with Your Holy Spirit. Because I am now Yours, I am willing to share what knowledge You have given me with others. Please empower me to do what You want me to do.

Confess: I am sorry for not being more in tune with Your desire and wishes for me. I humbly surrender my life to You. Use me in Your service, and I thank You for this opportunity.

Thank: Thank You, Jesus, for who You are. Thank You for being true to Your name. Thank You for helping me to seek for You. Thank You that Your light and truth will shine forth according to the desire of my soul. Thank You for helping me to continue to hunger and thirst after righteousness daily so that I can be filled.

Journal Entry

_____

_____

_____

_____

_____

_____

_____

_____

_____

_____

_____

_____

_____

_____

_____

_____

_____

_____

_____

Day 27

BE AN EAGER BEAVER
FOR GOD

The Holy Spirit came into the schools of the prophets, bringing even the thoughts of the students into harmony with the will of God. There was a living connection between heaven and these schools, and the joy and thanksgiving of loving hearts found expression in songs of praise in which the angels joined.

—*Ye shall Receive Power,*
by E. G. White, pg. 146

Can you believe that the Holy Spirit is willing to come into the school where you spend your days? He is willing to work with the teachers who cooperate with Him and with you. If you are in harmony with the Word and will of God through prayer, you have become a living connection between heaven and earth. Through you the Holy Spirit can come into your school or wherever you are and transform the lives of those around you. The Holy Spirit will teach you to become joyful and thankful, to have a loving heart and to sing songs of praise to God as you go about your day. The Holy Spirit will teach you how to use all of your strengths and talents to bring glory and honor to God.

Even though you are young, you should ask God for help in welcoming the Holy Spirit into your life and surroundings. Don't repress or push back the Holy Spirit, but encourage the Holy Spirit to become a vital part of your life.

Application

Can you think of a way that you can become an eager beaver for Christ?

Can you think of a way that you can be a positive witness for Jesus in your school or in your church?

ACT

Ask: Dear Jesus, please allow me to become an eager beaver for You, one who is swift to take Your Word wherever You tell me to take it. Help me to do it with the sweetness of the Holy Spirit so that it can take root in the lives of those whom I come in contact with.

Confess: I confess to You that I don't know what to expect when I give myself to You. I don't know how to do swift and beautiful things for You. I am willing, and just in case I am not, please help me to become willing.

Thank: I thank You for helping me to listen as You ask me to become an eager beaver for You. I ask You to allow the Holy Spirit to work in and through me today. I thank You for being my best friend and I love You and accept Your task for me today.

Journal Entry

_____

_____

_____

_____

_____

_____

_____

_____

_____

_____

_____

_____

_____

_____

_____

_____

_____

_____

_____

MY NEED FOR THE
MIND OF CHRIST

For who hath known the mind of the Lord, that
he may instruct him? But we have the mind of
Christ.

—1 Corinthians 2:16

As we experience conversion, the work of trans-
formation of character takes place and contin-
ues to go on. Our understanding is increased as we
become more obedient to God's Word. Not only does
God teach us to know "the mind of the Lord," He
gives us His mind and will; He makes it our own.
That is truly awesome! God is so good that He allows
our minds to develop through the guidance of the
Holy Spirit so that we can carry out His work.

Watch as the Holy Spirit develops in you the
kind of character that is in harmony with His life.
Before, you were powerless, but now your weakness

will begin to disappear, and you who were shaky will become steady and strong. Continual devotion will make your friendship with Jesus so close that you will "have the mind of Christ." You will become one with Jesus so that you can claim His soundness and strength of principle and His clearness of perception, which is wisdom from God the Father, the source of all light and understanding.

Application

Have you been growing in grace and in the knowledge of Christ daily? Ask God for the help that you need so that you can be strengthened day by day.

Regardless of where you are in school, ask Jesus to keep you in the school of Christ so that you can grow stronger and become more useful for Him.

ACT

Ask: Dear Jesus, please help me to have the mind of Christ on a moment by moment basis. It is not as easy as it seems, so I am depending on You to give me Your mind.

Confess: I confess that I did not understand that the highest type of learning is in the school of Christ. Forgive me and help me to stay connected with this school so that the Word of God can do remarkable things in my life.

Thank: I thank You for teaching me that "the opening of God's Word is followed by remarkable opening in strengthening a person's faculties; for the entrance of God's Word is the application of divine truth to the heart, purifying and refining the soul through the agency of the Holy Spirit" (*Ye shall Receive Power,* by E.G. White, pg. 58).

Journal Entry

_____

_____

_____

_____

_____

_____

_____

_____

_____

_____

_____

_____

_____

_____

_____

_____

_____

_____

_____

_____

ABIDING IN HIM DAILY

Abide in me, and I in you. As the branch cannot
bear fruit of itself, except it abide in the vine; no
more can ye, except ye abide in me.

—John 15:4

It is our duty to ask for the Holy Spirit to fill our
lives every day so that our sin sick souls can be
healed. Without Him, we are like a branch broken
off a tree: all we can do by ourselves is wither and
die. When we ask for the Holy Spirit He will get to
work on our minds, reconnecting us with God who
is our source of life and in whose presence we are
truly at home. In fact, the Holy Spirit will take His
healing even further and wake our hearts up to truth
that is free from error.

If you really want to know the truth, you will
not remain in ignorance. God rewards those who

diligently seek His precious truth. It is time for each one of us to feel the converting power of God's grace, so open your heart's door so that Jesus can come in. If for some reason you have closed your heart, plead with the Holy Spirit to open the door for you. Pray earnestly for Jesus to abide in you. Let us fall flat on our faces before the throne of divine grace, praying that God's Spirit may be poured out upon us as He was upon the disciples. The truth is, His presence will soften our hard hearts, and fill us with joy and rejoicing, transforming us into channels of blessing.

Application

Have you felt the necessity to be rich in faith, the kind of faith that is the fruit of the Spirit working upon the mind? It is time we ask for this living faith. Let's take the time to talk to Jesus about it.

Are you ready to have light shine into your minds so that you may become efficient workers for Him? Ask Him to do this for you now.

ACT

Ask: Dear Holy Spirit, please do not leave me without Your help because I need it. Please take the things of Christ and show them to me because I am seeking. Please help me to keep my eyes fixed on Jesus until I am conformed into His image.

Confess: I confess that I have taken my eyes off Jesus many times and failed because of it. Please forgive me and help me to be consistent in keeping my eyes on the prize.

Thank: Thank You, Jesus, for allowing the Holy Spirit to change me in spirit and purpose until I become one with You. Thank You for helping me to hunger and thirst after righteousness as my affection for Christ increases. Thank You for helping me to continue to behold Christ until I am changed from glory to glory, so that I will become more and more like the Master.

Journal Entry

_____

_____

_____

_____

_____

_____

_____

_____

_____

_____

_____

_____

_____

_____

_____

_____

_____

_____

_____

_____

STEP BY STEP VICTORY THROUGH PRAYERS

I therefore so run, not as uncertainly, so fight I, not as one that beateth the air; but I keep under my body, and bring it into subjection; lest that by any means, when I have preached to others, I myself should be a castaway.

—1 Corinthians 9:26, 27

God is so awesome! He leads his children, young adults, and older ones, step by step, every day. Even though life is sometimes like a battle and a march, He does not let us wear ourselves out; instead, He leads us gently on. So, my friends, keep running, keep fighting, for the battle is not yours, but God's. That should give each one of us courage to keep on going. In this Christian warfare there is no release; the efforts we make must be continuous, and we must keep persevering with God leading.

By these efforts through Christ the victory over the enemy can be maintained.

Because of your youth, God is calling upon you to be strong. With your relentless energy and determined purpose the victory is certain with Jesus. Jesus is calling you to have a disciplined mind, one that is educated and trained by the Holy Spirit. You see, there are hereditary and cultivated tendencies to evil that we must overcome. Hereditary tendencies are things we are born with, and for humans one of those tendencies is to do evil. Traits we do not inherit from our parents, we cultivate by what we allow our eyes to see and our ears to hear. If we cultivate a tendency to do wrong, it becomes easy for Satan to have his way with us, but with the Holy Spirit as our constant companion, step by step victory is certain.

Application

Have you made the choice to become a student in the school of Christ?

Write out a plan with Jesus asking Him to help you form habits of thought that will enable you to resist temptation. Ask Him for a step by step victory that will keep you in a trusting relationship with Him.

ACT

Ask: Precious Jesus, I am committed to You and I ask that You will give me the step by step victory that I need to keep me transformed into Your image and that I will be just like You on a daily basis.

Confess: I confess that I am slow in learning what You have to teach me. I confess my faults and ask Your forgiveness. Please teach me how to have You shine out of and through me each day.

Thank: I thank You for teaching me that I have no time to lose. Thank You for allowing me to know that probation will soon close. Thank You for teaching me that eternity stretches before us. Thank You for the knowledge that the curtain is about to be lifted and my precious Jesus is about to come. Thank You for the angels who are seeking to attract me from myself and from earthly things. By Your grace, I will not let them labor in vain (paraphrased from *Ye Shall Receive Power*, by E.G. White, pg. 68).

Journal Entry

_____

_____

_____

_____

_____

_____

_____

_____

_____

_____

_____

_____

_____

_____

_____

_____

_____

_____

_____

_____

_____

_____

Bibliography

Maxwell, Randy *If My People Pray,* Pacific Press Publishing Association, Boise, Idaho, Oshawa, Ontario, Canada – 1995.

White, E. G. *Child Guidance*, Southern Publishing Association, 1954.

White, E. G. *Ye Shall Receive Power*, Review & Herald Publishing Association, Hagerstown, MD.

About the Author

I have grown from a child of prayer to a praying adult. My mom taught me to pray both in deed and by example. At times I wondered why my mom was on her knees so long, but as I grew older, I understood that with ten children she had lots to talk to God about. I now believe that she must have known about the "ACT" formula to stay in such close connection with the God she loved.

I learned to trust God as her prayers were visibly answered before the eyes of her children. I felt His protection through prayer day and night growing up in a country filled with superstition. Because I learned so much, I would like to share how you can enjoy time with the same Jesus I have come to know.

I love Jesus very much because He helped me. I talk to Him a lot. He loves me and He loves you too. Talk to Him in prayer every day. Any good thing you crave He will help you to get if you do your part.

Here is a fun way to help you remember how to pray using the "ACT" formula:

A   Ask God for what you need
C   Confess—Say sorry when you do wrong
T   Thank Him for the good things He gives you

9 781414 111230